31

Day Promise
Prayer and Encouragement
Journal for
Parents and Caregivers of
Autistic Children

Written by
Donna Miles

This book belongs to

_____

To my autistic nephew, Johnie III, I love you.

To my children, Earnest III and Kimberley Sheri, I love you greatly.

You have given me a passion and a purpose.

To my late husband, Earnie, who always supported anything I've ever done.

To my late parents, Mildred and Johnie Sr., thank you for
teaching me to work hard and pursue my dreams.

To my siblings: Cassandra, Detra, Donna Lisa, and Johnie, Jr. keep praying and
interceding for all of those who hope in the Lord. The best is yet to come.

To the parents of autistic children, God has promised to carry you and
give you the added strength you need to keep on moving. You are very
special, for you were chosen to pass this test. May you have the strength
and love of Christ in your heart each day. You *can* and *will* endure.

Table of Contents

Introduction

What plans we have for our children! There is great excitement as we prepare for their arrival. What sorrow we may feel when our plans do not turn out as expected.

The demands of autistic children, many times, overwhelm us. When under tremendous stress, we may fail to consult God as we should. If you are feeling pressure, the prayers in this book may bring you comfort. Prayer really does change things. Although the situation may give you a heavy heart, prayer can change how you react to it.

God's promises are true and eternal. In our chaotic lives, it is easy to focus on our troubles instead of our blessings. God is so full of grace and mercy. These prayers challenge you to slow down a second and take notice of your blessings instead of your troubles. Many times, blessings come in disguise. The scripture comes straight from the Bible and informs you that if God brings you to it, he will take you through it! It's time to *pray*!

The journal entries will allow you to reflect on what you can do to strengthen your faith and help yourself and others.

The Autistic Child's Prayer

Dear God,

Protect me from the evils of life.

Carry me in times of enormous strife.

Place people in my path that will be kind to me.

Send lots of love my way and help me to be all that I can be.

Provide me with teachers, health-care providers, and friends who have that special touch.

Bless everyone who interacts with me and loves me so much!

Amen.

The Autistic Child's Parents' Prayer

Heavenly Father,

I come to you with a sincere heart.

Stay close beside me and never depart.

Strengthen, lead, and guide me to help my child each day.

Build me up when I am down and show me the way.

I may never understand while this test is mine to be,

But hold me close when I feel weak and grant me wisdom throughout eternity.

Show me that miracles can lie in the power of prayer.

Give me faith that never ends when my soul is in despair.

When I feel that hope is of no avail,

Speak to my heart and remind me that your love never fails.

Amen.

The Autistic Child's Teachers' Prayer

God, bless me to be a teacher full of love,

Lead me and guide me, and send angels to protect me from above.

Give me the wisdom to teach those students sent to me.

Gird up my strength to push my students to be all that they can be.

Help me to communicate and work with parents and service providers each day.

When times get rough and I feel discouraged, please show me the way.

I ask for patience and understanding when things seem to go wrong.

Clear my mind, help me speak kind words, and keep my body strong.

In the name of Jesus, I pray.

Amen.

Autism Acrostic

A is for Awesome (Give me a chance, I really am Awesome!)

U is for Understanding I am different (Please give me your Understanding)

T is for Tailor Made (God made no one else like me, for I am unique and Tailor-Made))

I is for important (My life is as Important as anyone else)

S is for SAVED (I am Saved and made whole by the blood of Jesus)

M is for Magnificent (Give me your love and patience so that I may feel Magnificent)

Let's encourage everyone to embrace the uniqueness and differences in all of mankind.

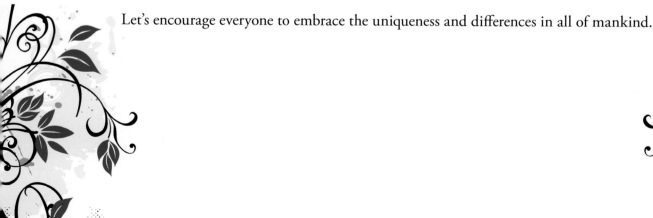

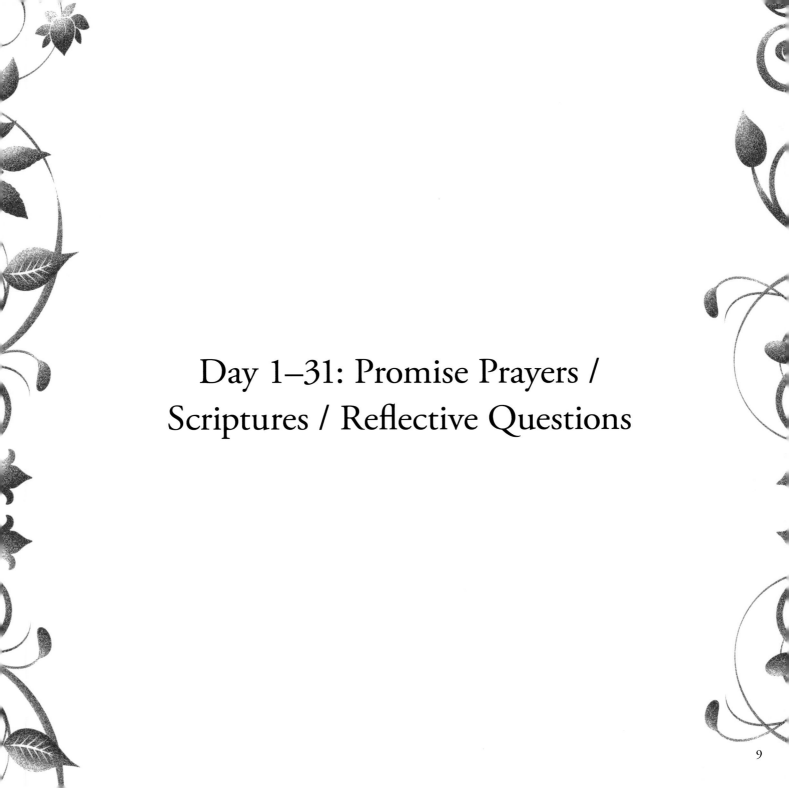

Day 1–31: Promise Prayers /
Scriptures / Reflective Questions

Day 1

Heavenly Father,

Comfort me when I feel stressed.

Give me a peace that only you can give.

Remind me of all the beautiful reasons why I live.

Amen.

<u>Scripture: Psalm 55:22</u>

"Cast all your cares on the Lord and he will sustain you: he will never let the righteous fall."

Daily Reflection: What cares do I need to cast on the Lord today?

_____

_____

_____

_____

_____

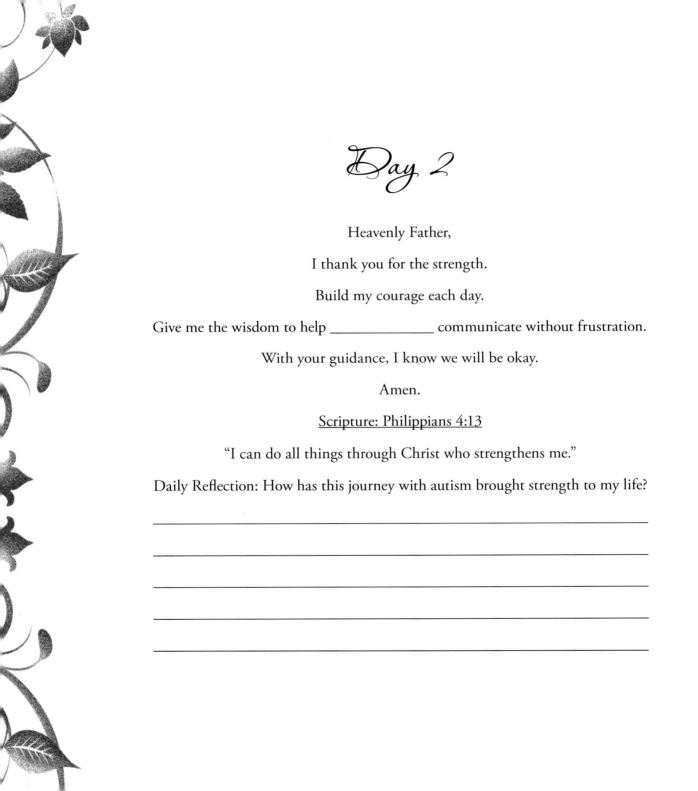

Day 2

Heavenly Father,

I thank you for the strength.

Build my courage each day.

Give me the wisdom to help _____ communicate without frustration.

With your guidance, I know we will be okay.

Amen.

Scripture: Philippians 4:13

"I can do all things through Christ who strengthens me."

Daily Reflection: How has this journey with autism brought strength to my life?

_____

_____

_____

_____

Day 3

My Savior, my Lord,

Please be my guide.

Saturate me with your grace and mercy.

Give me peace of mind this hour.

Bless me and my family and keep us within your power.

Amen.

<u>Scripture: John 14:27</u>

"Peace I leave with you, my peace I give unto you: not as the world giveth, give I unto you. Let not your heart be troubled, neither let it be afraid."

Daily Reflection: Am I really at peace, or am I troubled and afraid?

_____

_____

_____

_____

_____

Day 4

Dear Lord,

Walk with me through this test.

Open my eyes to see only the best.

Help me grow stronger in my faith because of this.

The words of the Bible I will never dismiss.

<u>Scripture: 1 Corinthians 16:13</u>

"Watch ye, stand fast in faith, quite like men, be strong."

Daily Reflection: What do I need to do to strengthen my faith?

_____

_____

_____

_____

_____

Day 5

Precious Heavenly Father,

Guide me according to your will.

Give me courage and help me to keep still.

Cover (name of child) with your precious love.

Place people in our lives to help us like angels from above.

Amen.

Scripture: Psalm 121:1

"I will lift up mine eyes unto the hills from whence cometh my help."

Daily Reflection: How can I lift up someone who needs encouragement today?

_____

_____

_____

_____

_____

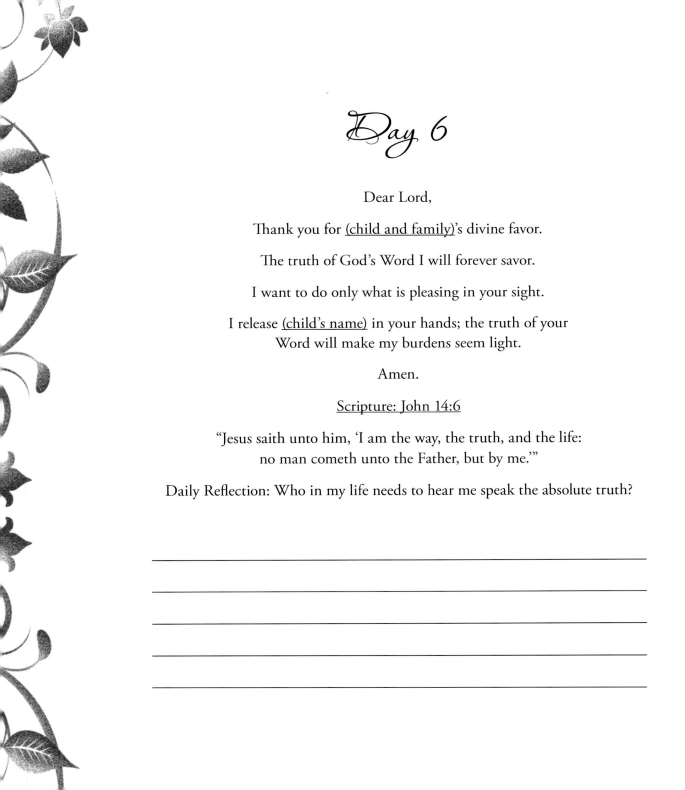

Day 6

Dear Lord,

Thank you for (child and family)'s divine favor.

The truth of God's Word I will forever savor.

I want to do only what is pleasing in your sight.

I release (child's name) in your hands; the truth of your
Word will make my burdens seem light.

Amen.

Scripture: John 14:6

"Jesus saith unto him, 'I am the way, the truth, and the life:
no man cometh unto the Father, but by me.'"

Daily Reflection: Who in my life needs to hear me speak the absolute truth?

_____

_____

_____

_____

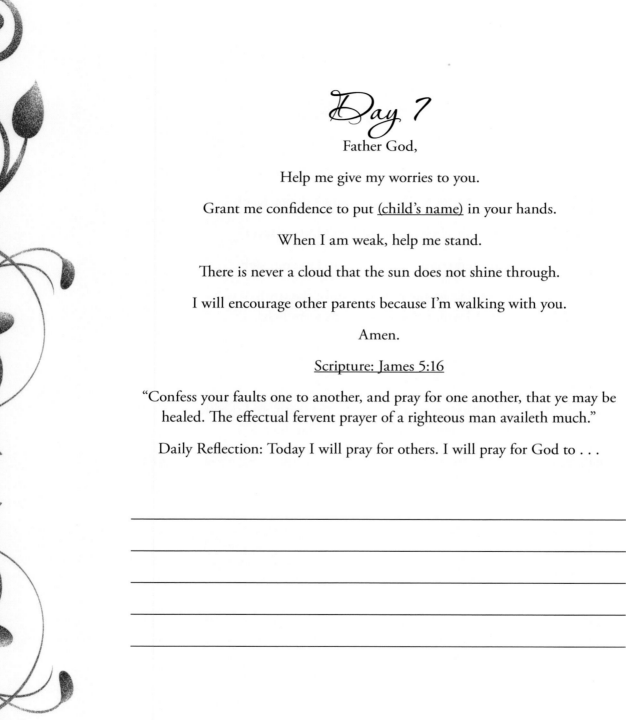

Day 7

Father God,

Help me give my worries to you.

Grant me confidence to put (child's name) in your hands.

When I am weak, help me stand.

There is never a cloud that the sun does not shine through.

I will encourage other parents because I'm walking with you.

Amen.

Scripture: James 5:16

"Confess your faults one to another, and pray for one another, that ye may be healed. The effectual fervent prayer of a righteous man availeth much."

Daily Reflection: Today I will pray for others. I will pray for God to . . .

_____

_____

_____

_____

_____

Day 8

Dear God,

Stir up creativity in me.

Clear my vision so that I may see what it is that you want me to see.

I want to help others who are experiencing this same test.

I thank you for the strength to do my very best.

Amen.

Scripture: Psalm 31:24

"Be of good courage, and he shall strengthen your heart, all ye that hope in the LORD."

Daily Reflection: How will I help others who are experiencing this same test?

_____

_____

_____

_____

_____

Day 9

Most Gracious Father,

When my day starts to go south, help me turn to you.

Your grace and power are such that I can never ask for too much!

I will pray and continue to pray, for I know God is real.

I will intercede for other families, for it is God's will.

Amen.

Scripture: James 1:6

"But let him ask in faith, nothing wavering. For he that wavereth is like a wave of the sea driven with the wind and tossed."

Daily Reflection: Today I will ask God to help me . . .

_____

_____

_____

_____

_____

Day 10

Father,

Thank you for working through my weaknesses.

I admit that many days I don't feel very strong.

Your Word promises that your power is made perfect in my weakness.

If I keep your promise in my heart, I know I can't go wrong.

Amen.

Scripture: Luke 11:9

"And I say unto you, ask, and it shall be given you; seek, and ye shall find; knock, and it shall be opened to you."

Daily Reflection: What promise has God declared that I should remind myself of daily to keep me strong?

_____

_____

_____

_____

_____

Day 11

Lord,

I thank you for my child.

My heart has been softened and humbled through this experience.

I will continue to sow and sow and sow,

For the seeds that I am planting are helping me to grow and grow and grow.

Amen.

Scripture: Psalm 126:5

"They that sow in tears shall reap in joy."

Daily Reflection: What seed will I sow today that will help me grow?

_____

_____

_____

_____

_____

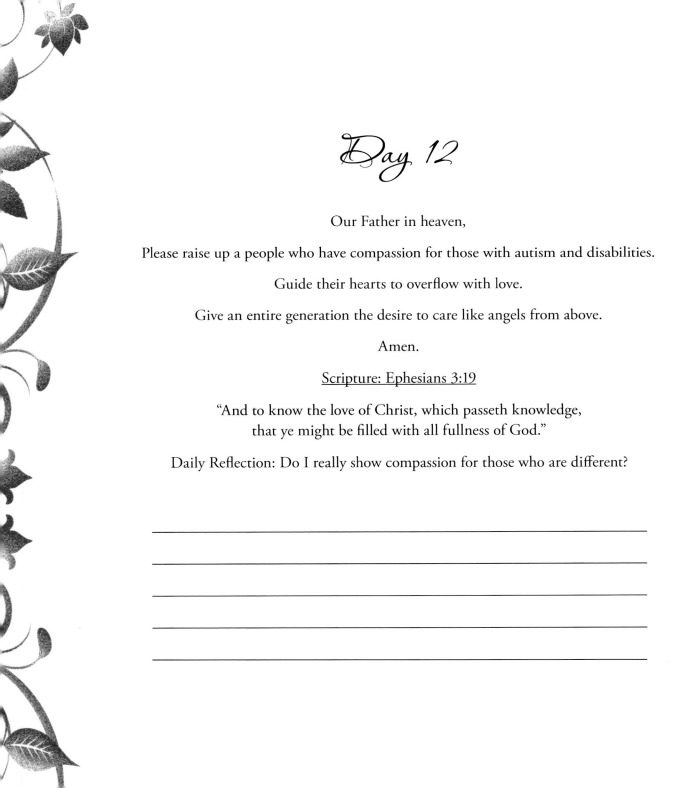

Day 12

Our Father in heaven,

Please raise up a people who have compassion for those with autism and disabilities.

Guide their hearts to overflow with love.

Give an entire generation the desire to care like angels from above.

Amen.

Scripture: Ephesians 3:19

"And to know the love of Christ, which passeth knowledge,
that ye might be filled with all fullness of God."

Daily Reflection: Do I really show compassion for those who are different?

_____

_____

_____

_____

_____

Day 13

Dear God,

No matter how many challenges I face today,

I refuse to be discouraged.

I will count my blessings and not focus on my worries.

Amen.

<u>Scripture: Ephesians 1:3</u>

"Blessed be the God and Father of our Lord Jesus Christ, who hath blessed us with all spiritual blessings in heavenly places in Christ."

Daily Reflection: Today I will think about and list my blessings.

_____

_____

_____

_____

_____

Day 14

Most Gracious Father,

When my day starts to go south, help me turn to you.

Your grace and power are such that I can never ask for too much!

Amen.

<u>Scripture: Colossians 3:16</u>

"Let the word of Christ dwell in you richly in all wisdom; teaching
and admonishing one another in psalms and hymns and spiritual
songs, singing with grace in your hearts to the Lord."

Daily Reflection: What song can I sing that will uplift me when I am down?

_____

_____

_____

_____

Day 15

Dear God,

I will praise you when I'm up and praise you when I'm down.

Bless my eyes and ears to see all the joy my family brings to me.

I will strive to be content and work hard to follow your plan.

When I am feeling low, never let go of my hand.

Amen.

Scripture: Psalm 118:24

"This is the day that the Lord has made; we will rejoice and be glad in it."

Daily Reflection: How can I really rejoice in the Lord?

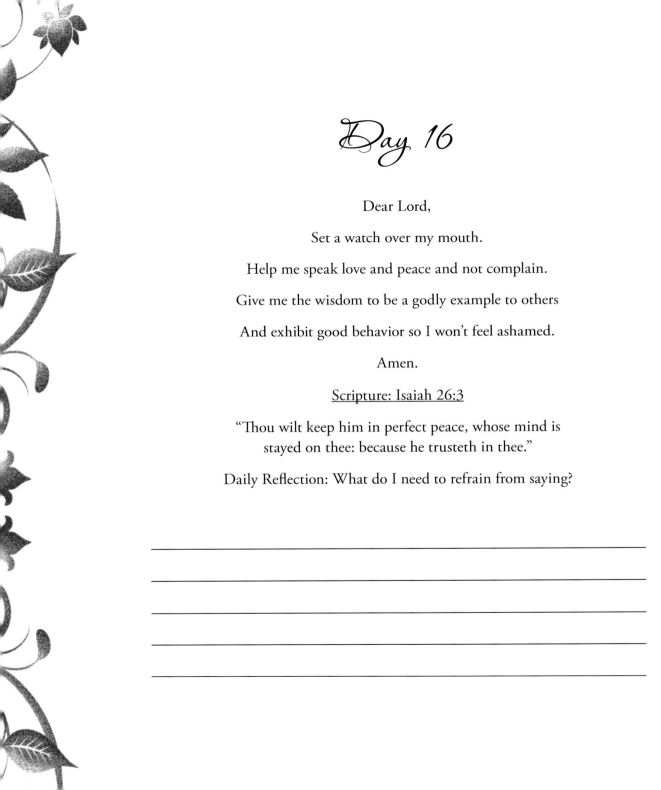

Day 16

Dear Lord,

Set a watch over my mouth.

Help me speak love and peace and not complain.

Give me the wisdom to be a godly example to others

And exhibit good behavior so I won't feel ashamed.

Amen.

Scripture: Isaiah 26:3

"Thou wilt keep him in perfect peace, whose mind is stayed on thee: because he trusteth in thee."

Daily Reflection: What do I need to refrain from saying?

_____

_____

_____

_____

_____

Day 17

Our Father in heaven,

Open my eyes that I may see your grace and feel your presence close to me.

When you send angels to help me and my child,

Give me discernment so that I may recognize.

Amen.

<u>Scripture: Psalm 121:1</u>

"I will lift up mine eyes unto the hills from which cometh my help."

Daily Reflection: How can I slow down to hear and recognize when God is speaking to me?

_____

_____

_____

_____

_____

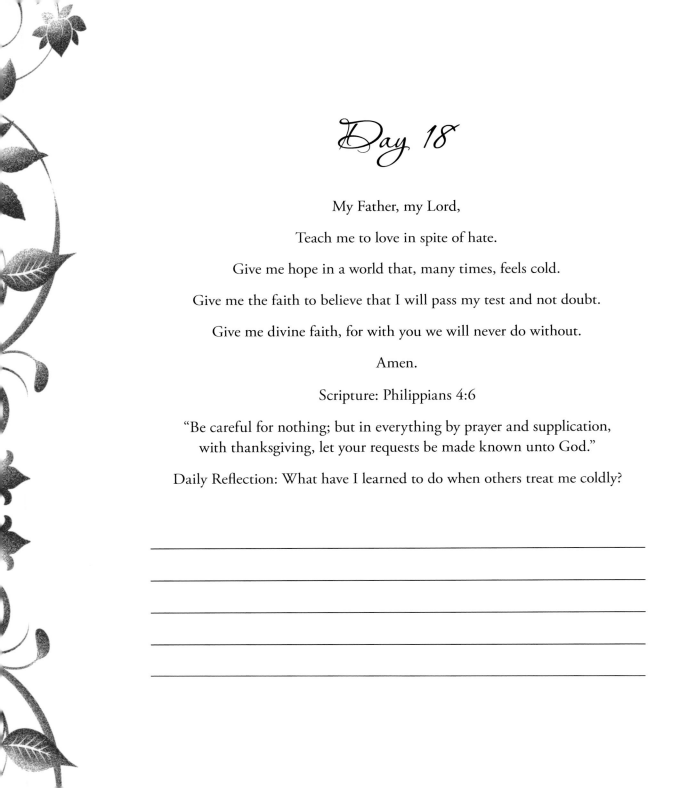

Day 18

My Father, my Lord,

Teach me to love in spite of hate.

Give me hope in a world that, many times, feels cold.

Give me the faith to believe that I will pass my test and not doubt.

Give me divine faith, for with you we will never do without.

Amen.

Scripture: Philippians 4:6

"Be careful for nothing; but in everything by prayer and supplication, with thanksgiving, let your requests be made known unto God."

Daily Reflection: What have I learned to do when others treat me coldly?

_____

_____

_____

_____

Day 19

Heavenly Father,

Forgive my doubtful ways,

Keep me strong, and put purpose in my days.

When I am disappointed and shed tears,

Enable me to see how you have blessed me throughout the years.

Amen.

<u>Scripture: Psalm 147:3</u>

"He healeth the broken in heart, and bindeth up their wounds."

Daily Reflection: Today I will list how God has blessed me through this experience.

_____

_____

_____

_____

_____

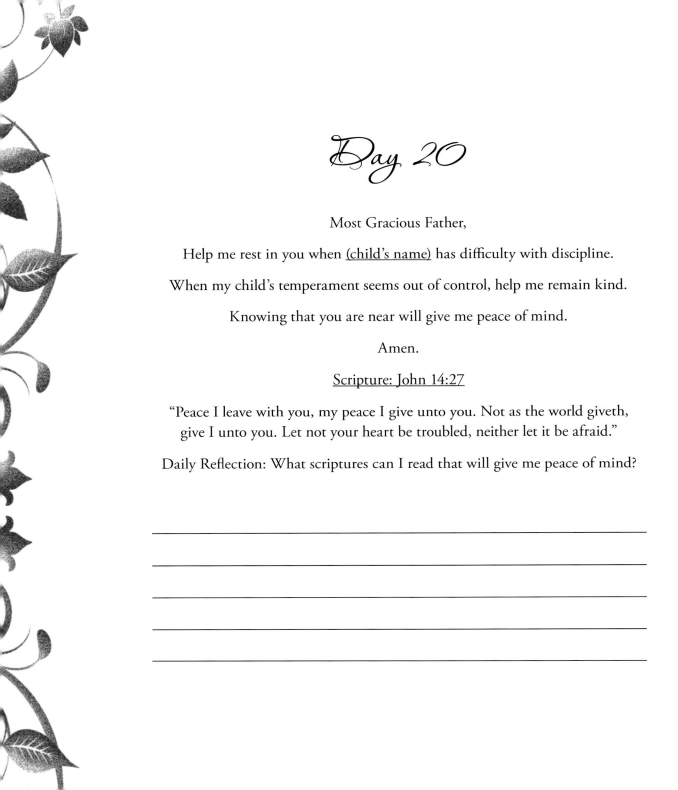

Day 20

Most Gracious Father,

Help me rest in you when <u>(child's name)</u> has difficulty with discipline.

When my child's temperament seems out of control, help me remain kind.

Knowing that you are near will give me peace of mind.

Amen.

<u>Scripture: John 14:27</u>

"Peace I leave with you, my peace I give unto you. Not as the world giveth, give I unto you. Let not your heart be troubled, neither let it be afraid."

Daily Reflection: What scriptures can I read that will give me peace of mind?

_____

_____

_____

_____

_____

Day 21

Thank you, Lord, for giving me the ability to be a good parent/caregiver.

Help me stay encouraged and feel the glory of your power.

I need your grace and mercy each and every hour.

Amen.

<u>Scripture: Matthew 21:22</u>

"And all things, whatsoever ye ask in prayer believing, ye shall receive."

Daily Reflection: What prayer will I pray to God and believe that I will receive it?

_____

_____

_____

_____

_____

Day 22

Father God,

Remind me that your grace is sufficient when people seem to stare.

Keep my mind strong when I am in despair.

I pray for your guidance, for you know what we need.

Keep my mind clear so that I may let you lead.

Amen.

<u>Scripture: 2 Corinthians 9:8</u>

"And God is able to make all grace abound to every good work."

Daily Reflection: How will I keep my mind strong when I feel despair?

_____

_____

_____

_____

Day 23

Dear God,

Give me hope when others treat us coldly.

Send us true friends that will treat us like pure gold.

Show us the power of love when I call on your name.

Help me spread autism awareness, for no one is to blame.

Amen.

<u>Scripture: Psalm 31:24</u>

"Be of good courage, and he shall strengthen your heart, all ye that hope in the Lord."

Daily Reflection: What can I do to spread autism awareness in my community?

_____

_____

_____

_____

Day 24

Father in heaven,

Today as I work with my child, I will do so in the name of Jesus.
Help me encourage my child to try new nutritious foods.

I pray that he/she learns to adjust to transitions in a positive way.

Give me a vast measure of happiness; in my mind the Word of Jesus will stay!

Amen.

<u>Scripture: Proverbs 3:13</u>

"Happy is the man that findeth wisdom, and the man that getteth understanding."

Daily Reflection: Today I will introduce my child to a new food. We will try . . .

_____

_____

_____

_____

_____

Day 25

Most Gracious Father,

Sometimes the stress of the day leaves me weary and blue.

Renew my energy; give me comfort and a joy that man cannot understand.

Keep my family in the hollow of your hand.

Amen.

Scripture: Proverbs 17:22

"A merry heart doeth good like a medicine, but a broken spirit drieth the bones."

Daily Reflection: What joy do I have that the world has not given me?

_____

_____

_____

_____

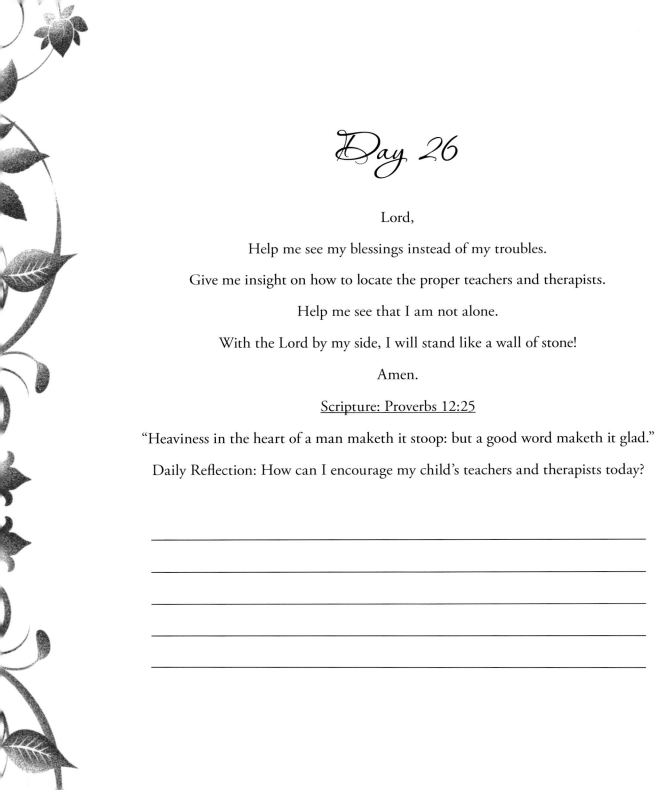

Day 26

Lord,

Help me see my blessings instead of my troubles.

Give me insight on how to locate the proper teachers and therapists.

Help me see that I am not alone.

With the Lord by my side, I will stand like a wall of stone!

Amen.

Scripture: Proverbs 12:25

"Heaviness in the heart of a man maketh it stoop: but a good word maketh it glad."

Daily Reflection: How can I encourage my child's teachers and therapists today?

_____

_____

_____

_____

Day 27

Dear Lord,

I will keep hope in my heart.

Teach me how to pray for my child.

Lead me to the right doctors and caregivers.

Grant me the gifts of faith and love from within.

I do not ask for an easy hill to climb.

With your love in my heart, I am sure that *victory* is *mine*!

Amen.

<u>Scripture: Psalm 71:14</u>

"But I will hope continually, and will yet praise thee more and more."

Daily Reflection: When the feeling of hopelessness dwells
in my heart, I will cry out to the Lord for . . .

_____

_____

_____

_____

_____

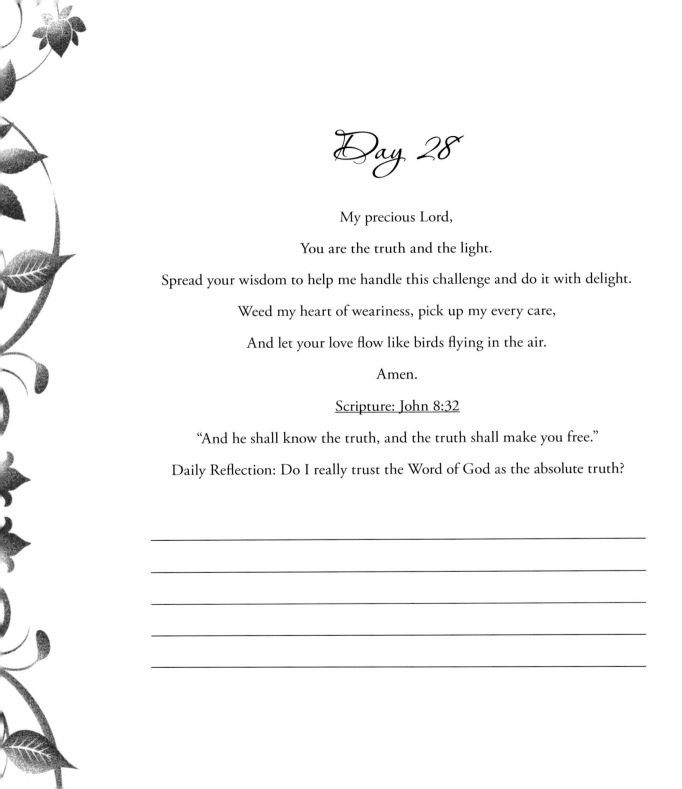

Day 28

My precious Lord,

You are the truth and the light.

Spread your wisdom to help me handle this challenge and do it with delight.

Weed my heart of weariness, pick up my every care,

And let your love flow like birds flying in the air.

Amen.

Scripture: John 8:32

"And he shall know the truth, and the truth shall make you free."

Daily Reflection: Do I really trust the Word of God as the absolute truth?

_____

_____

_____

_____

Day 29

Lord,

Make me a man/woman of wisdom.

Help me be a godly parent.

I realize that I can't be a good parent without you.

Give me techniques to help <u>(child's name)</u> make sense of the world as each day passes by.

For your glory, <u>(child's name)</u> will make progress in the twinkling of an eye.

Amen.

<u>Scripture: James 3:17</u>

"But the wisdom that is from above is first pure, then peaceable, gentle, easy to be entrusted, full of mercy and good fruits, without partiality, and without hypocrisy."

Daily Reflection: How can I use prayer and the Word of God to make me a woman/man of wisdom?

_____

_____

_____

_____

_____

Day 30

Master,

I will praise you through every stage in my life.

Take away my impatience and irritability—I refuse to live in strife.

Give your angels charge to protect my family wherever we go.

To those with autism and disabilities, love and kindness I will always show.

Amen.

Scripture: Psalm 104:33

"I will sing unto the Lord as long as I live. I will sing
praise to my God while I have my being."

Daily Reflection: I will elevate my praise to God today by . . .

_____

_____

_____

_____

_____

Day 31

My Savior, my Lord,

You know the desires of my heart.

Help me be kind and long-suffering.

Magnify my strength to always do my part.

I rebuke the spirit of tantrums and defiant behavior and release the spirit of calm.

I confess the promises in your Word, Lord, and believe that angels will keep us from harm.

Amen.

Scripture: Jeremiah 33:3

"Call unto me, and I will answer thee, and show thee great
and mighty things, which thou knowest not."

Daily Reflection: What does my heart really desire? What miracle will I pray about today?

_____

_____

_____

_____

_____

Prayer Tips for the Autistic Child's Parent or Caregiver

We live in a society that moves quickly. We do everything in a hurry. We must learn to set aside some time for our Savior each day. As humans, we will experience problems and heavy burdens. Many times, there is no one who can help us but the Lord. Let's practice giving our burdens to him. The Word states that he will carry us in times of enormous stress. The Lord is the only one that can give us joy and peace in the midst of a storm.

1. Set aside time to pray for you and your child every day. (There is power in prayer.)

2. Don't skip praying; make prayer a priority. (Stop to pray. Pray in your car, in the bathroom, or just steal away for a few minutes.)

3. Know that the Lord cares for you and your family. (For God *so* loved the world that he gave his only begotten son.)

4. Get a prayer partner or pray with other people. (So many people want to pray but don't know how to ask.)

5. Place prayer books and a Bible in a place where you can see them daily. (Make Christian materials easily available.)

6. Listen to Christian music and watch Christian television. (Keep your mind stayed on Jesus. If Satan gets in your mind, you will begin to doubt, worry, and become weak.)

7. Set aside at least five minutes to meditate daily. (This can be done in the shower or during lunch.)

8. Believe that your prayers will be answered. (Your prayers are being heard by a mighty God. God is bigger than any problem or situation that you face!)

Watch your mouth! What you say often hinders your belief that the situation will work out postively. State positive confessions over you and your family each day. Your mind and attitude will be strengthened.

Daily Confessions

1. (Name of child) and I walk in the favor of God every day.

2. (Name of child) is protected by angels every day.

3. (Name of child) is loved by all who works with him/her.

4. Caregivers and service providers will treat (name of child) kindly, lovingly, and gently.

5. (Name of child) is blessed and will learn to the best of his/her ability.

6. (Name of child) will develop a pleasing temperament.

7. (Name of child) will develop strategies to communicate with others effectively.

8. (Name of child) will learn to transition from one routine to another without melting down.

9. (Name of parent/caregiver) is happy and healthy.

10. (Name of parent/caregiver) refuses to doubt and worry about this journey with autism.

11. The Lord will send Christian help from the north, south, east, and west.

12. This journey with autism will bring me and those around me closer to the Lord.

Pray for thirty-one days. See the power of God in one month. The thirty-one short, easy-reading prayers and scriptures allow you to meditate and reflect on God's promises as you walk through this journey with autism.

If we go to God in prayer about our tests instead of complaining to our friends and creating more stress, we can see the power of God at his *best*!

It's time for spiritual warfare—pray!

Slow down a bit and draw close to God. Pray about this journey with autism. Give God thirty-one days and see the changes that prayer will bring into your life.

Printed in the United States
By Bookmasters